PENGUINS

with
People Problems

A PERIGEE BOOK

PENGUINS
with
People Problems

∿∿∿

Mary Laura Philpott

A PERIGEE BOOK
Published by the Penguin Group
Penguin Group (USA) LLC
375 Hudson Street, New York, New York 10014

USA • Canada • UK • Ireland • Australia • New Zealand • India • South Africa • China

penguin.com

A Penguin Random House Company

PENGUINS WITH PEOPLE PROBLEMS

ISBN: 978-0-399-17309-7

This book has been registered with the Library of Congress.

First edition: June 2015

PRINTED IN THE UNITED STATES OF AMERICA

10 9 8 7 6 5 4 3 2 1

Text design by Tiffany Estreicher

Most Perigee books are available at special quantity discounts for bulk purchases
for sales promotions, premiums, fund-raising, or educational use. Special books, or book
excerpts, can also be created to fit specific needs. For details, write:
Special.Markets@us.penguingroup.com.

To Matt Damon, as always.

Hello. Please, have a penguin.

If you're saying to yourself, "Good heavens, Wanda, these birds look like they were finger-painted by a four-year-old," you are correct, Wanda. They do. I'm no artist.

I'm just a writer. That's what I do for a living. The other thing I do for a living is read books—which is why I happened to be paying attention when Penguin Books and Random House announced their merger a few years ago. Like pretty much everyone else, I thought "Random Penguin" would be a great name for the new company. Unlike everyone else, I started doodling and captioning penguins doing random things and couldn't stop. Thus, "The Random Penguins" Tumblr was born.

The birds took on a life of their own once I started posting them online. They made a lot of friends in a short time, perhaps because they are rather people-ish. They make mistakes. They do stupid things. Just like people, they sometimes try (and usually fail) to hide their insecurities. And like even the most flawed people, they're lovable in spite of—or because of—all that. Well, most of them are. Some of them are real dirtbags.

A few of them are me. Are any of them you?

Enjoy,
Mary Laura

There was tacit agreement among Liam's friends that although the combination of his body type and his new striped sweater made him look like a bowling pin, no one would say anything, as his breakup with Denise had left him feeling very vulnerable.

Jerry is that jackass who, whenever someone introduces someone else as "my partner," always responds, "in crime?"

*N*either can remember the other's name, but neither can break down and ask, for they have been introduced to one another on eleven other occasions.

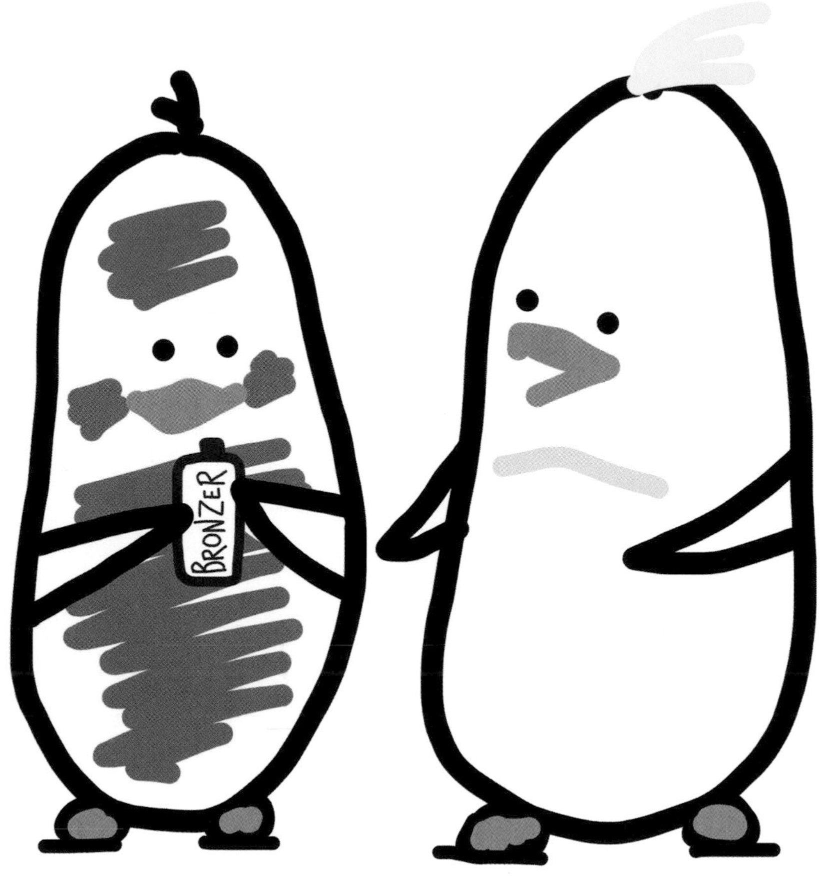
BRONZER

"No, it looks really natural. Like you just got back from the islands."

Ellie told her hot new boyfriend that she really enjoyed the crumpets on her last trip to England, and then he said he played the crumpet in his high school band, and then she said, "Shhhh . . . let's not talk."

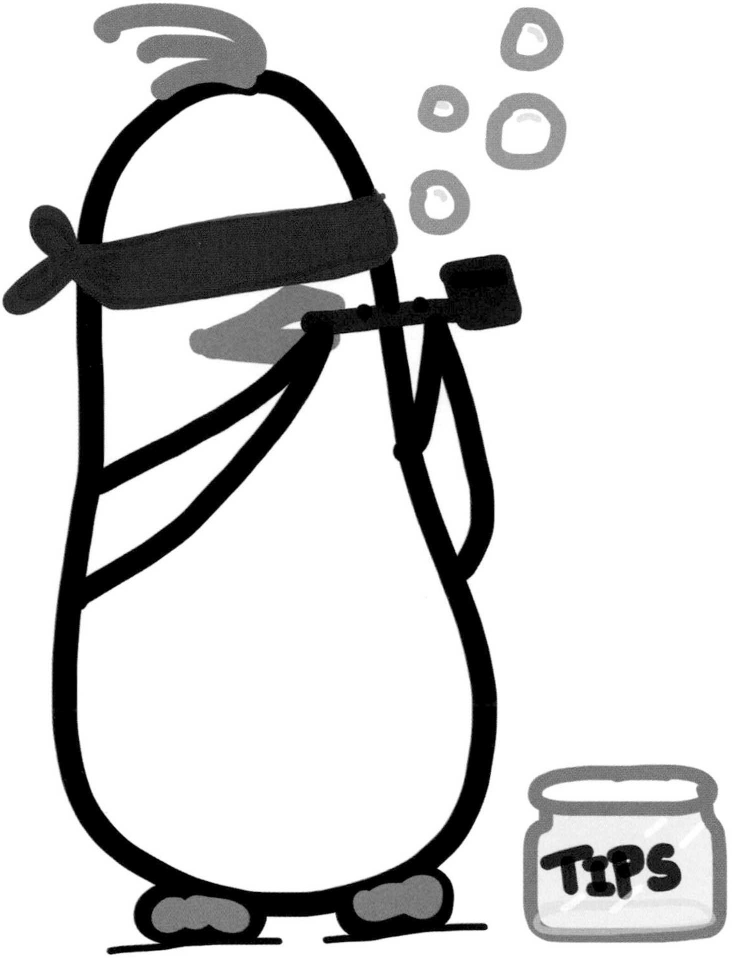
TIPS

"Choose a career that doesn't feel like work," they said. "Do what you love, and the money will follow," they said.

So for twenty-three years, Kevin's been out here blindfolded, playing the musical bubble pipe, waiting to get rich.

Waiting.

Still waiting.

Some raised their eyebrow-feathers at Joel and Phillip and said they were odd. But they didn't care. Love is love.

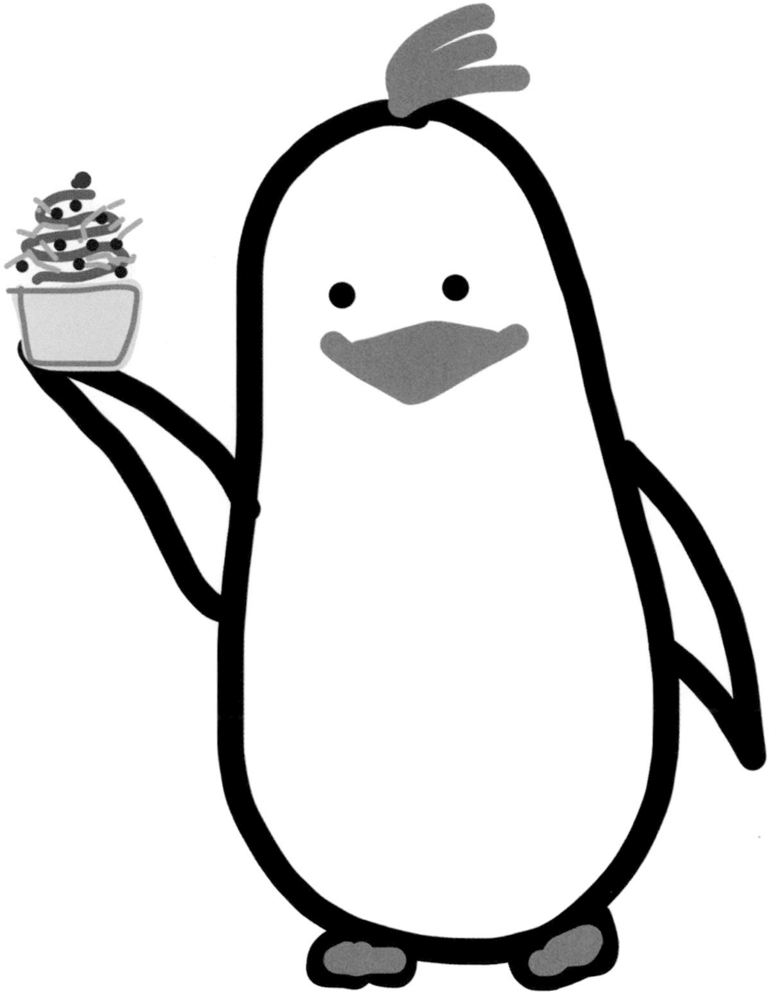

After a breakup, Karla takes extra-special care of herself, making time to do healthy things. For example, today for lunch, she's having a cup of organic Greek yogurt . . . topped with Oreos, Gummi snakes, coconut, M&M's, and caramel sauce—a dish she calls "Suck it, Brian."

Grande extra-sweet decaf Mocha Swirl:	$4.99
Tip to barista to write "Coffee—Black" on the cup:	$2
Maintaining a reputation:	Priceless

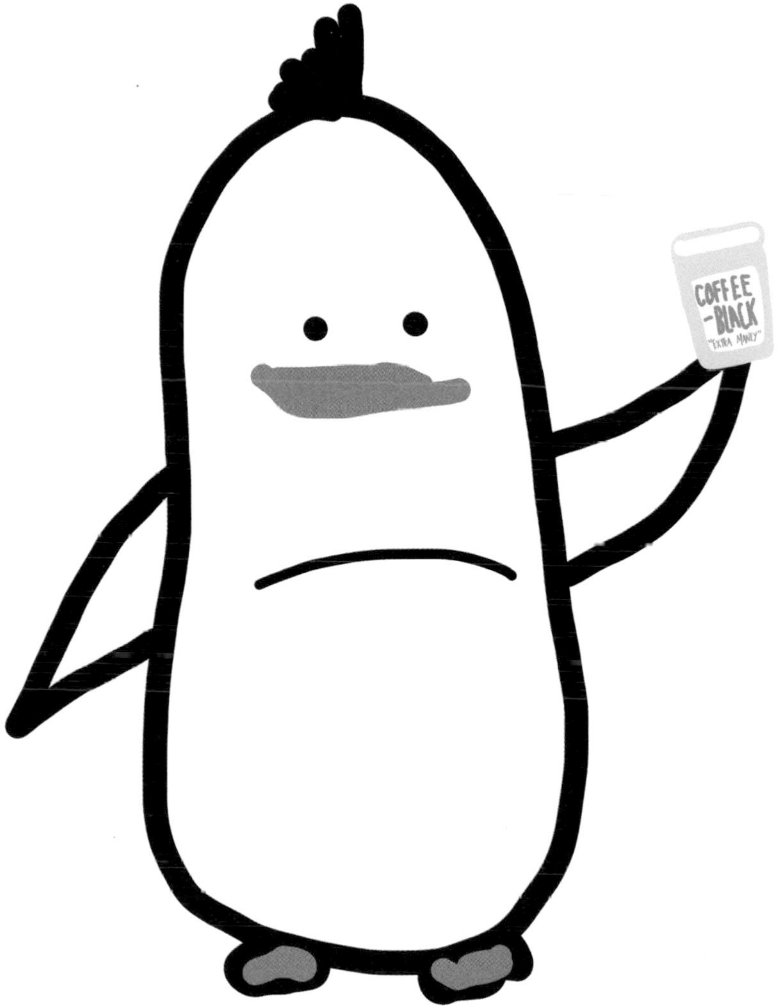
COFFEE
-BLACK
"EXTRA MANLY"

*H*onestly, sometimes Nicole likes getting ready for the party more than the party itself.

Maxine knew that her friendly American habit of smiling at strangers could be misinterpreted in other cultures as a lascivious invitation, so she tried to curb it when she traveled abroad. Problem was, she never remembered until she was halfway into a smile, at which point she'd just panic and freeze.

So mostly she went around looking like this

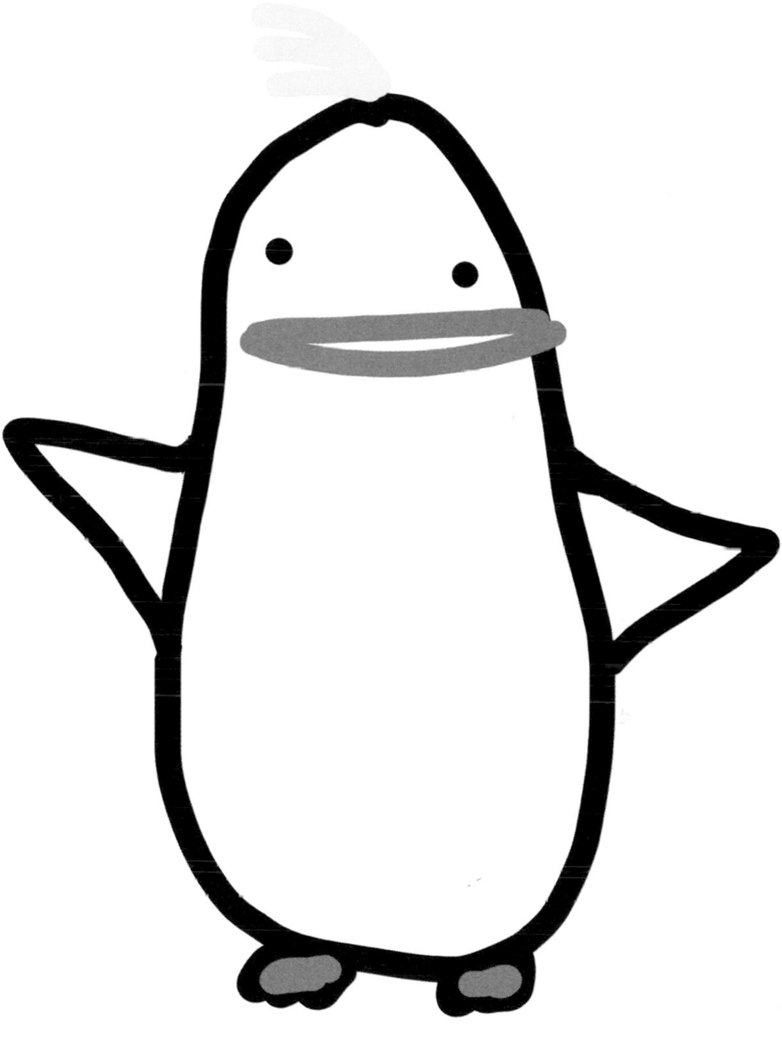

Well, that didn't turn out at *all* like those bitches on Pinterest said it would.

Happiness tip: Think of all the sounds around you as part of the cheerful soundtrack to the movie about your life.

For example, when you're shaking your purse to find your keys, and you can hear them but not see them, just imagine there's a tiny bluegrass band in there and someone's really going to town on the tambourine.

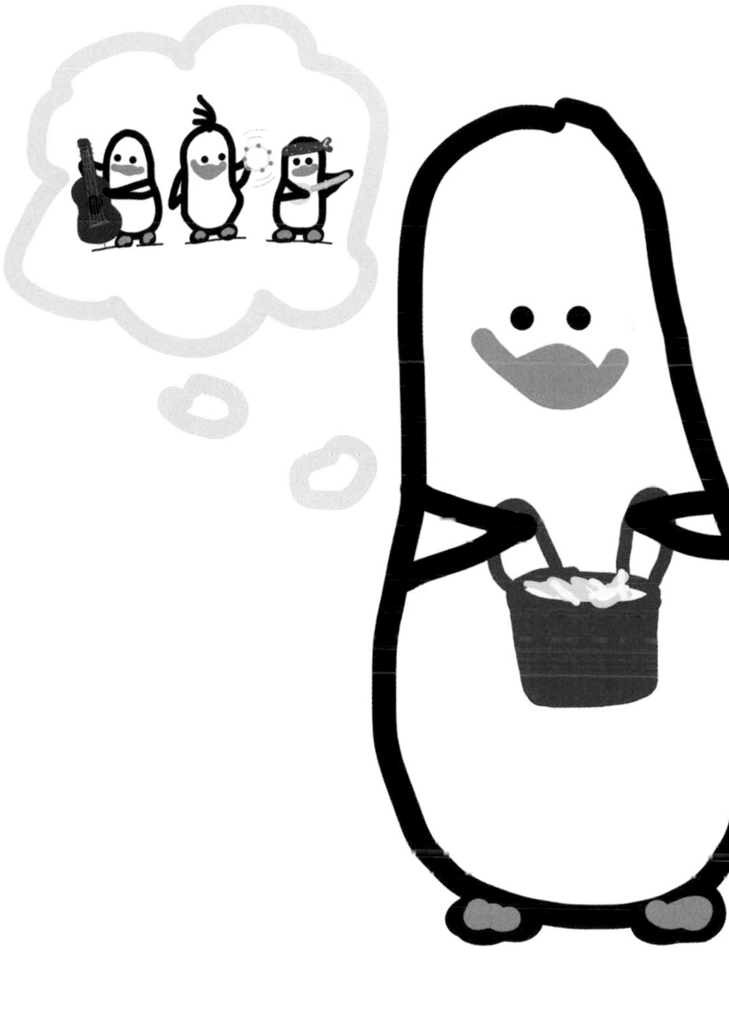

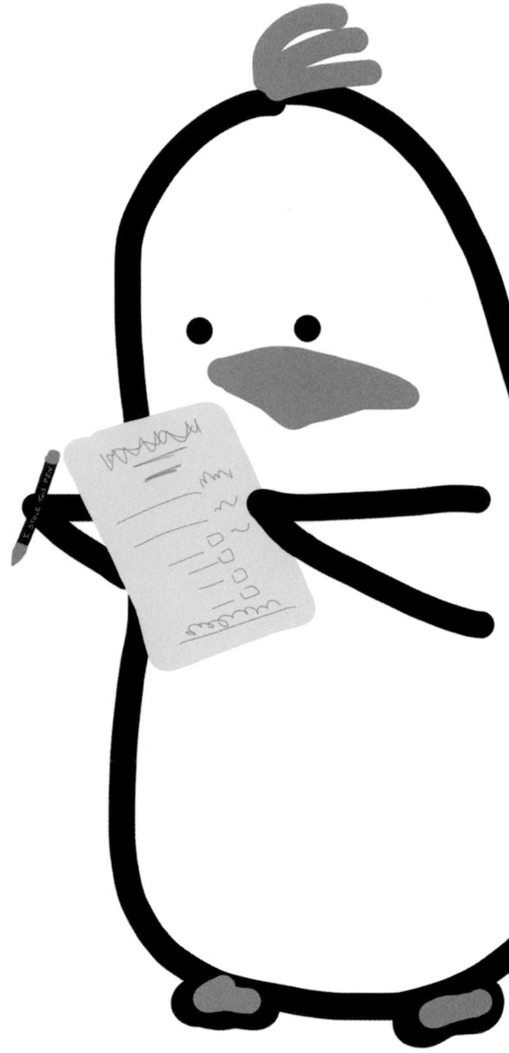
I STOLE THIS PEN

The health insurance form had four options for the "How often do you drink?" question: *daily, weekly, rarely,* and *never*—but she always had to write in:

"Usually twice a week, but some weeks more like daily, and sometimes at brunch if it's Saturday, but then after that none for about a week, and once none for a whole summer, but then ten in one day that time I ran over my neighbor's cat and tried to bury it and got sick and threw up on it and then the neighbor came outside and I was barfing on his dead cat."

Tina's been trying to stop cursing so much, but honestly, it's not going so damn well.

There's a whole special zone in Hell for waiters who ask, *"And would we be interested in dessert?"* in front of children.

This is a penguin whose coworker took his good pen and replaced it with some crappy pen.

He's about to go on a super-cute flippity-flappity rampage.

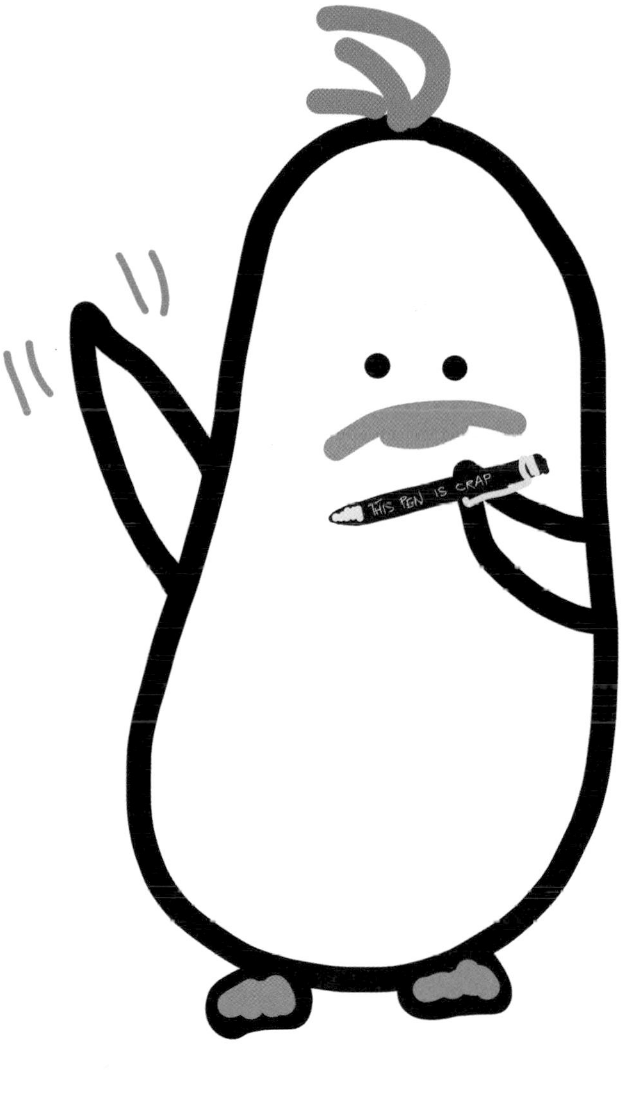
THIS PEN IS CRAP

Used to be, Penny had to lick the entire tray of muffins to claim them all for herself. Nowadays, all she has to do is shout "GLUTEN!" and everyone scatters.

*E*veryone has their talents. Stacie's is that she can make a near-perfect unicorn shadow on the wall.

Bee in the car.

"You're smart. You're powerful. You're in control of this situation. You know who you are? You're MARGARET SASSYBRITCHES THATCHER," is what he was saying to himself in the restroom mirror when his coworker walked in.

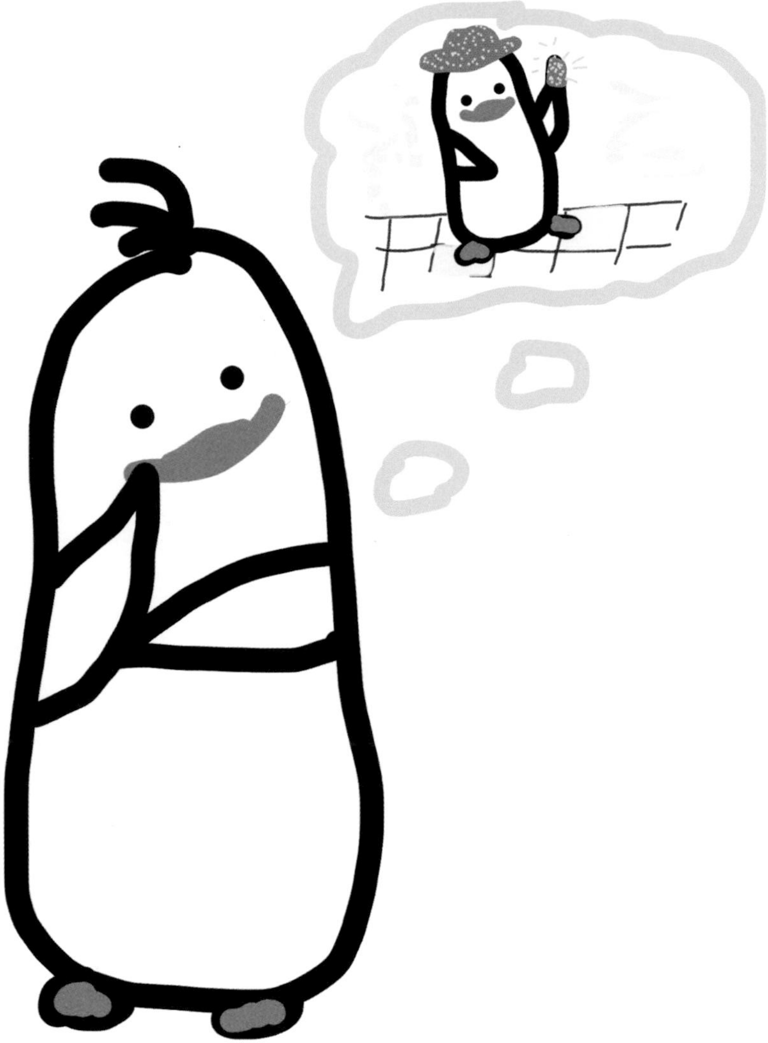

During job interviews, Milo answers the "What's your biggest weakness?" question with, "A chronic obsession with and desire to obtain a light-up floor just like the one in Michael Jackson's 'Billie Jean' video," revealing that in fact his true weakness is neither greed nor his love of sweet '80s dance tunes, but too much honesty.

Saw a YouTube tutorial about how to do a "smoky eye." Nailed it.

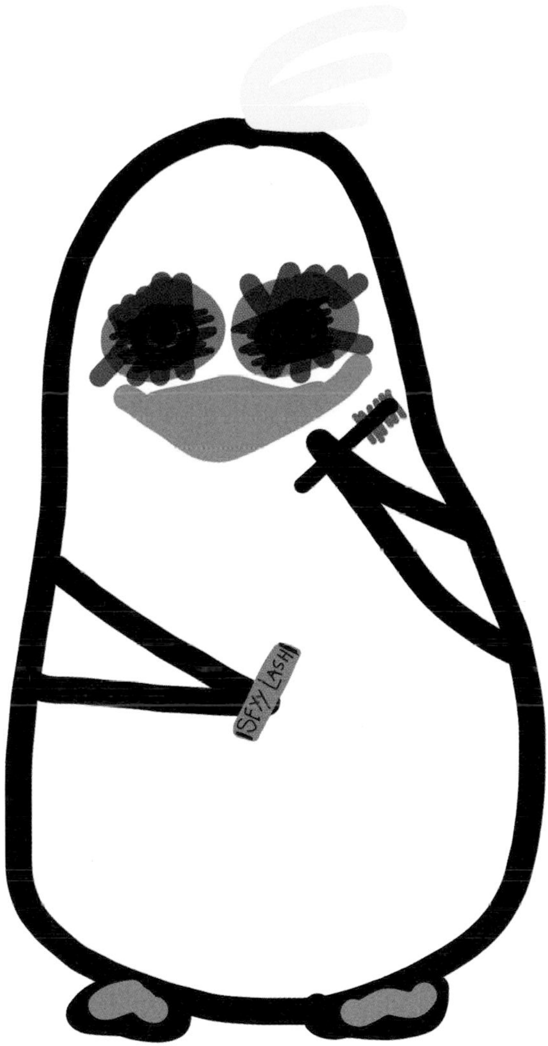
SEXY LASH

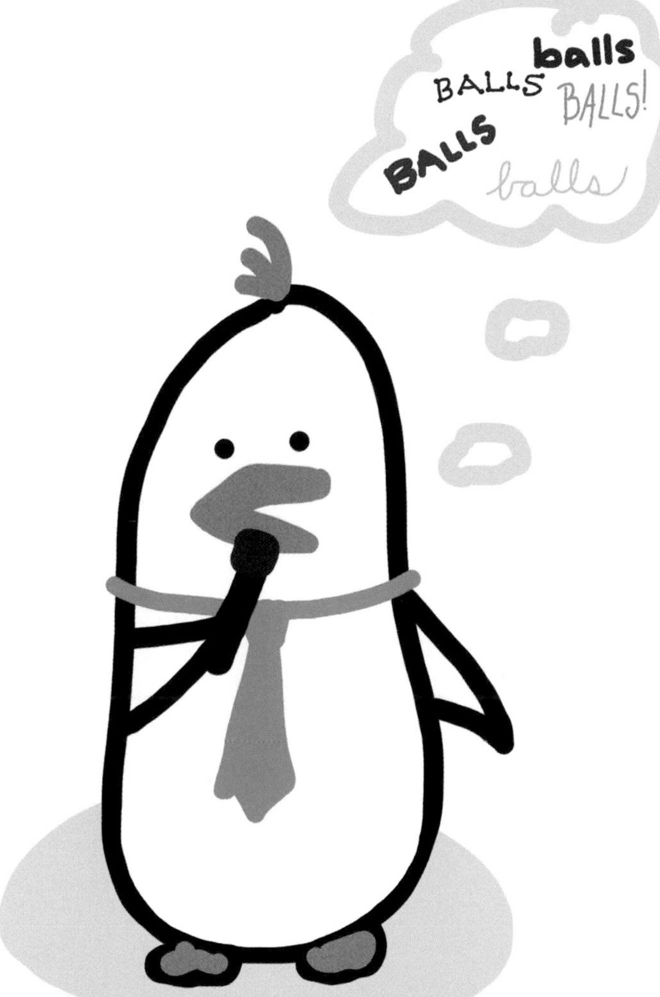
balls
BALLS
BALLS!
BALLS
balls

Rufus is going to journalism school to be a sportscaster. Not because he loves sports, but because he has thousands of ball jokes the world needs to hear.

Martha didn't know why she'd just blurted out the thing about her ovaries. But she did know two facts: (1) She was very, very bad at small talk. (2) The guy from the fifth floor would probably take a different elevator from now on.

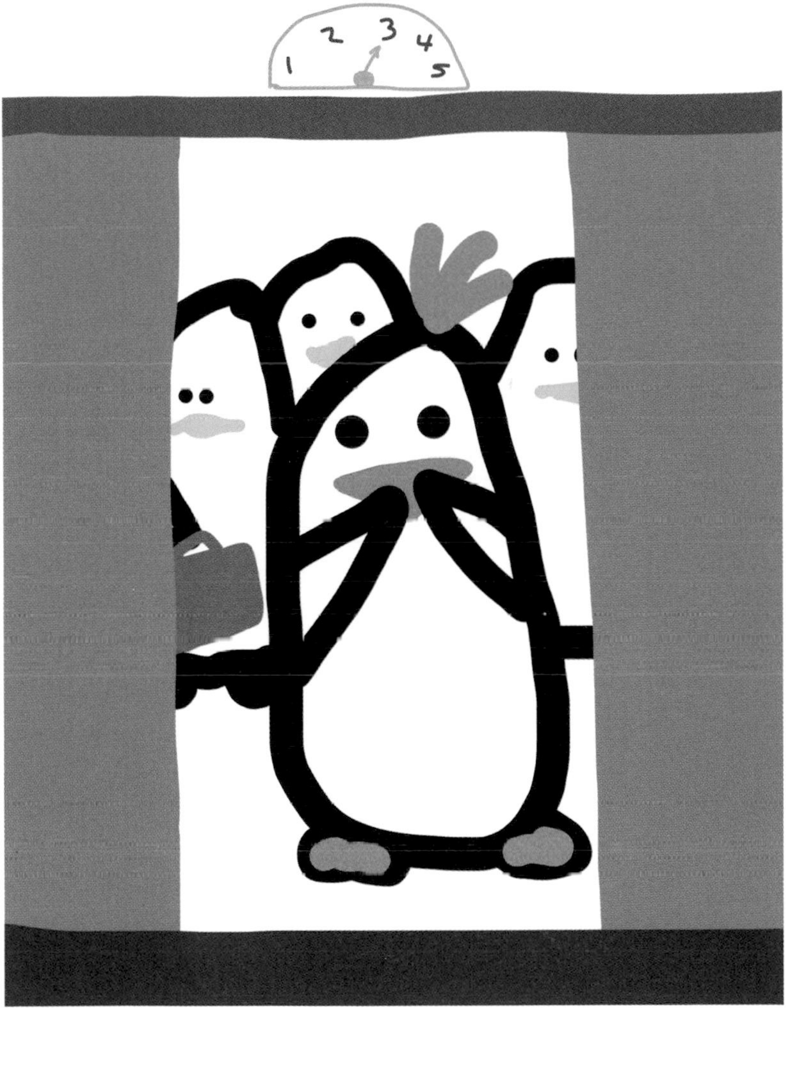
1
2
3
4
5

Leonora had already gotten a stern look from her boss twice, but she couldn't help it. If twirly chairs weren't for twirling, then WHY DID GOD MAKE THEM TWIRLY?

Angela was trying to do that hot-librarian thing where she whipped off her glasses, but she forgot she was wearing her specs on a chain and got all tangled up. Poor Angela. Failing at sexy . . . again.

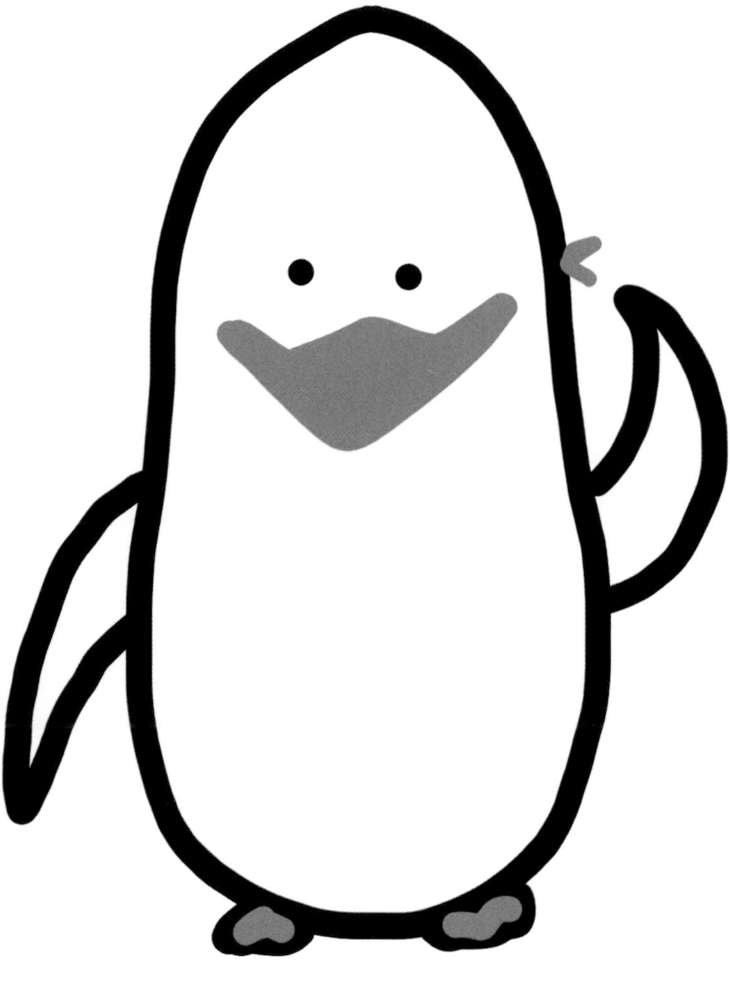

If there's one thing Phoebe's proud of, it's her strong public speaking skills.

If there are two things Phoebe's proud of, they're her strong public speaking skills *and* the tiny extra beak on the side of her head.

The problem with these flappy little wings is they can reach only so far with the sunscreen.

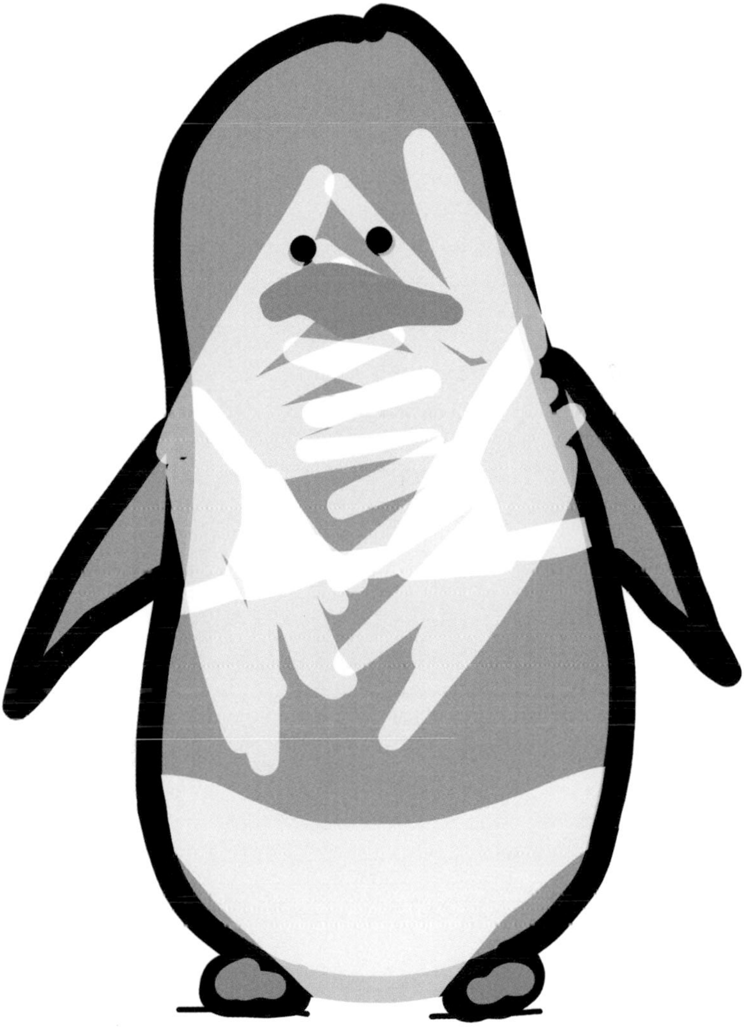

The important thing isn't who changed Daddy's profile picture to a butt wearing glasses—it's who's going to show Daddy how to change it back.

Ollie is Jeff's work-best-friend and Robert's work-best-friend *and* Lindsey's work-best-friend. He's a bit of a work-friend-whore, actually.

Stumped by the abstract, Ferdinand never really knew what to say about contemporary art. But he could fake it with any of the following:

"Wow. The energy."

"Oh, that's unexpected."

"Color!

Stop kicking me under the conference table.

lol k

Quit it.

lolololz

It's not lol, dumbass. Stop.

lol k sry

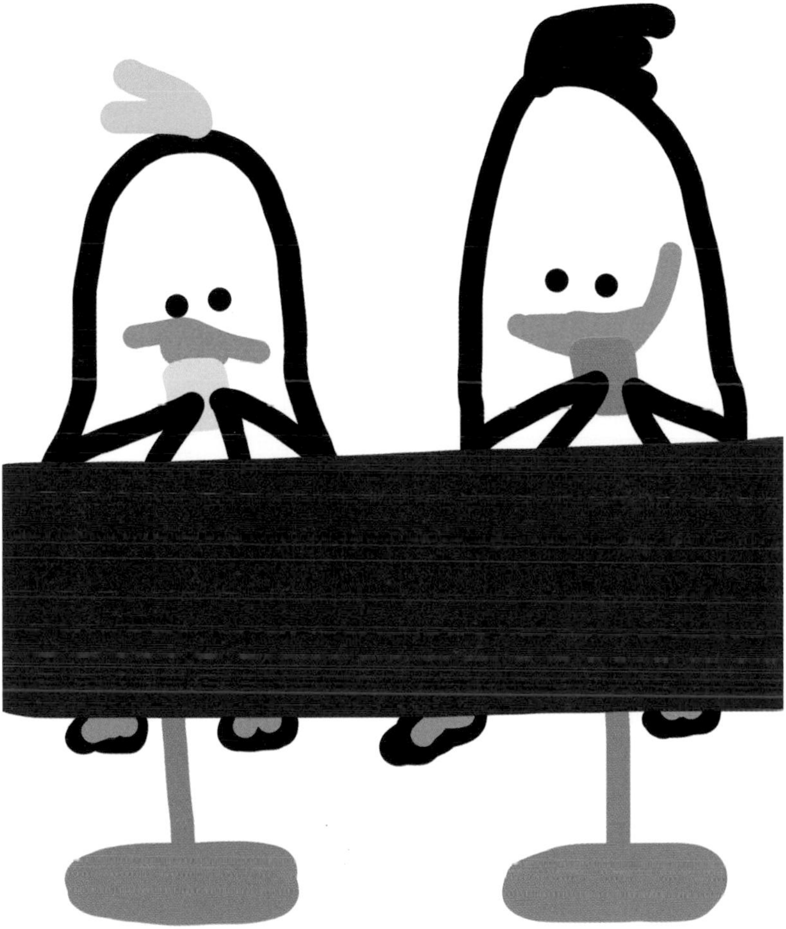

She's going to stab herself in the ears if her
grandmother says "pantyhose" one more time.

Back to work! But first coffee. And email. And some tunes and a bunch of fake news stories and top 10 lists and OMG LOOK AT THE UNLIKELY BABY ANIMAL FRIENDS IN THIS VIDEO. I DID NOT EXPECT A TIGER AND A MARMOSET TO SNUGGLE LIKE THAT! But *then*, back to work.

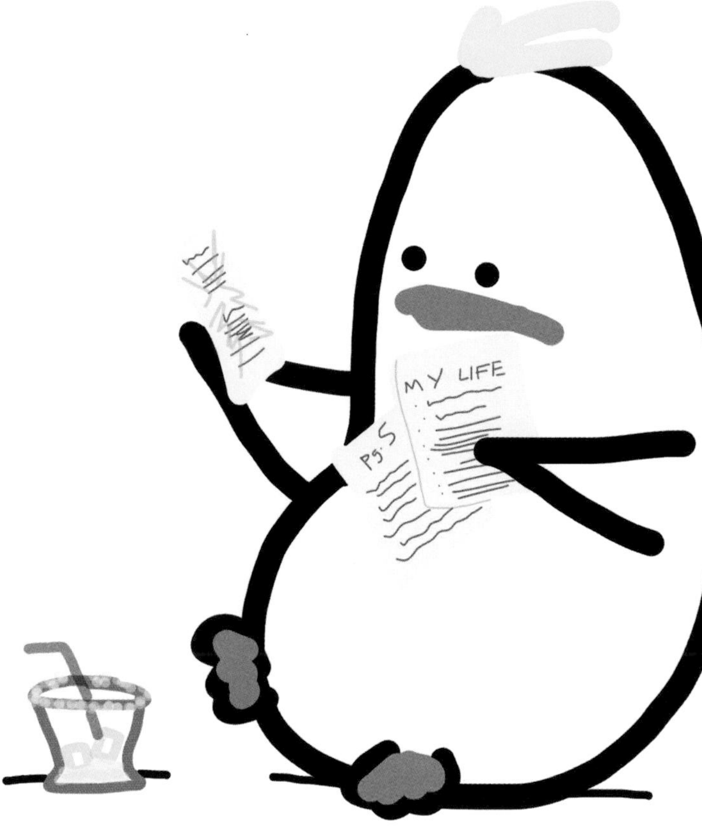
MY LIFE
Pg: 5

Natasha had four margaritas and then decided to start writing her memoir.

It needs a bit of editing.

"Is it too much to ask to have my basic needs met? Must I struggle LIKE SOME KIND OF ANIMAL? WHAT SORT OF EXISTENCE IS THIS?" he screamed when his wi-fi signal flickered again.

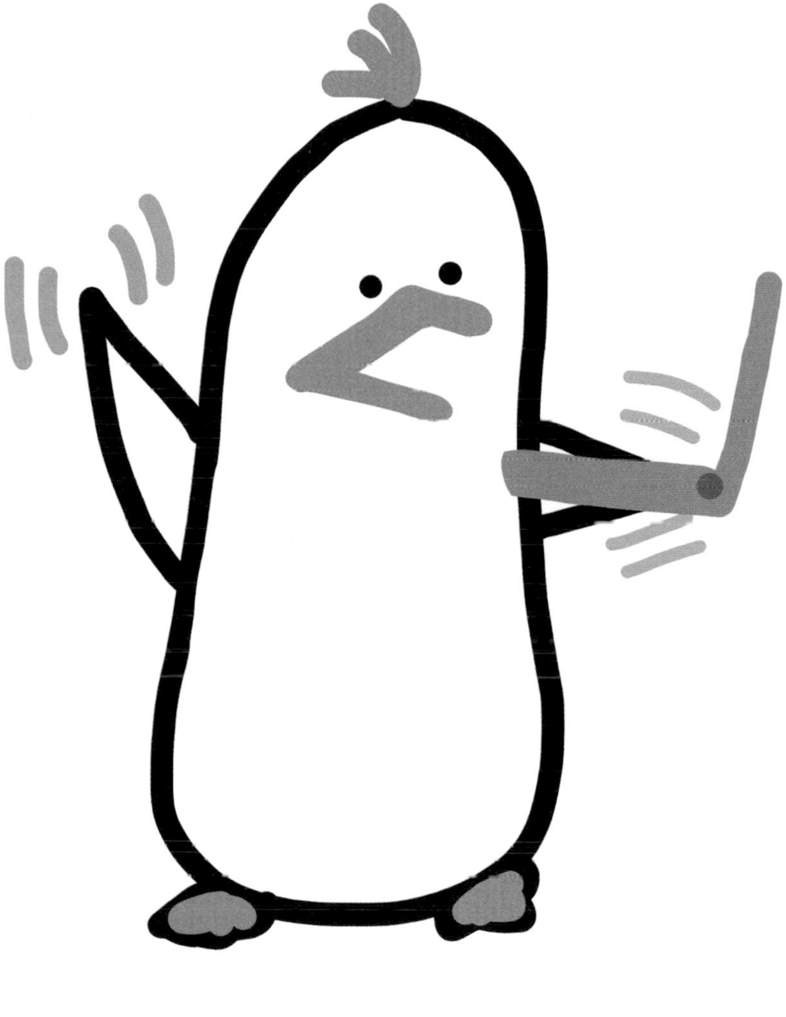

Spike follows his passions as an artist; and by "follows his passions," he means "smokes a lot of weed"; and by "artist," he means "perpetually unemployed person."

Also, by "Spike" he means "Gary."

This is that guy at work who'd be kind of funny if he weren't going overboard with the innuendos all the time. Like, yeah, Bob, we get it—it's a bagel, it has a hole in it.

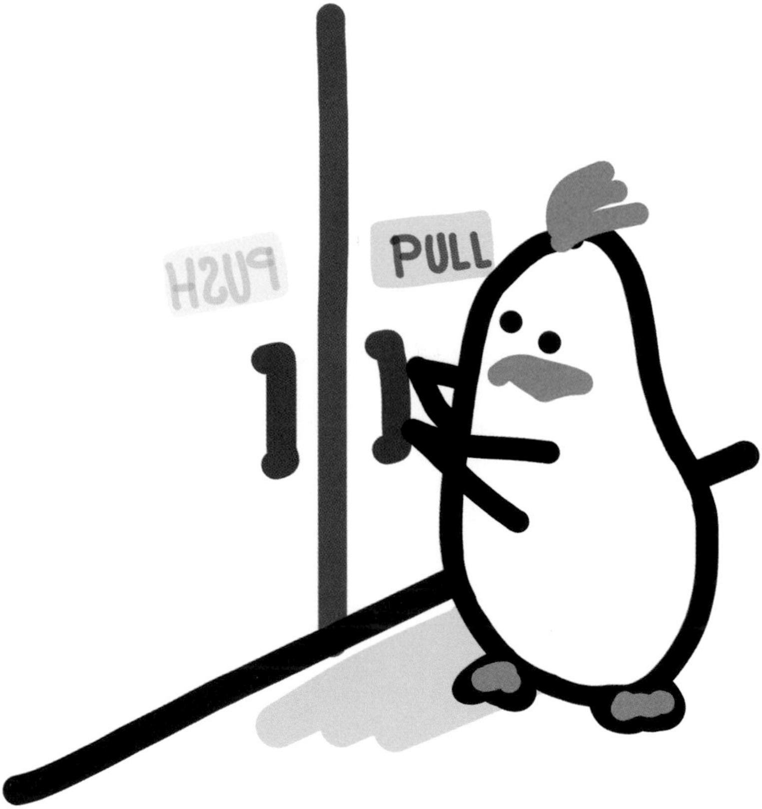
PUSH
PULL

Word problem:

James has tried to push open the door marked "Pull" eleven times in one week. How many more times will he do this before he starts parking on the other side of the building and using a different entrance because this door is stupid?

When Sam found *xcvbnm u89ihj l;k* in the middle of a paragraph he was writing, he realized it was time to drop a few pounds, because he was gut-typing again.

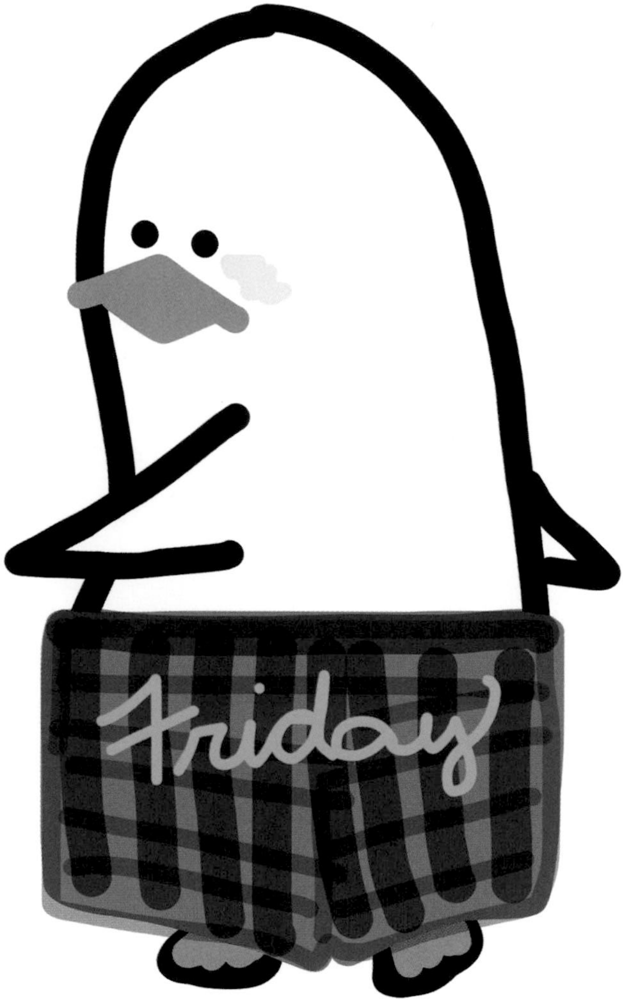
Friday

As Brad stripped down to his skivvies for his doctor's appointment, he felt a deep sense of shame, for he was wearing Friday . . . and it was Monday.

"Nope, I totally can't tell you got extensions."

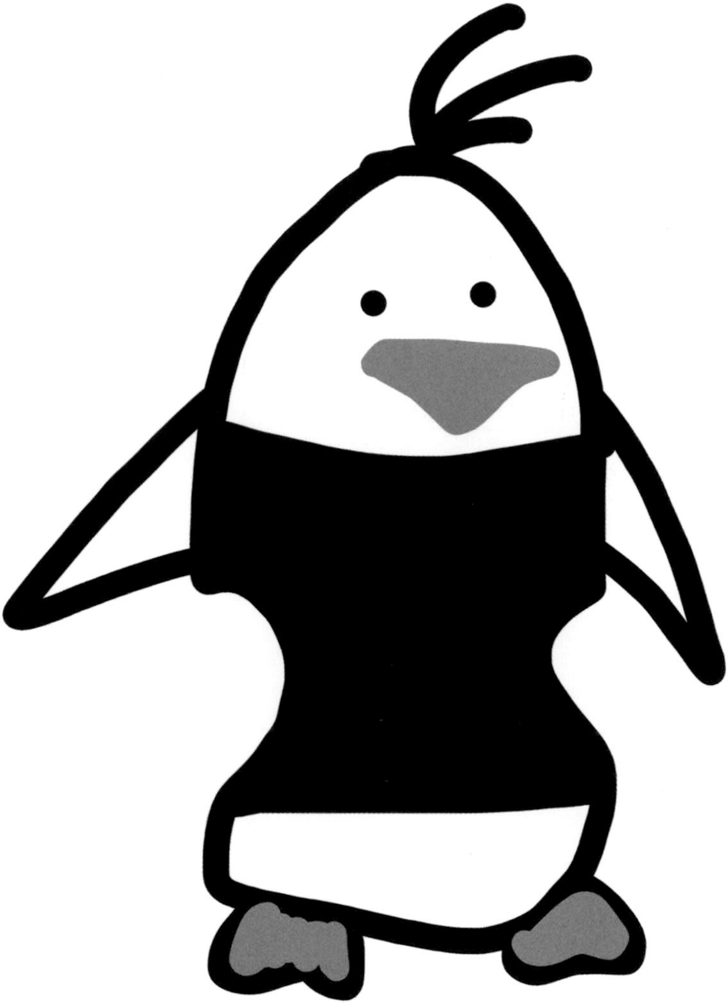

"My friends all rave about Spanx. Personally, I don't wear them. But my friends do."

Oh, Mike. That scraggly assortment of feathers on your face doesn't say, "I naturally grew this super-manly beard." It says, "Sometimes I feel a creeping sense of desperation about myself," and "Does this make me seem likable?"

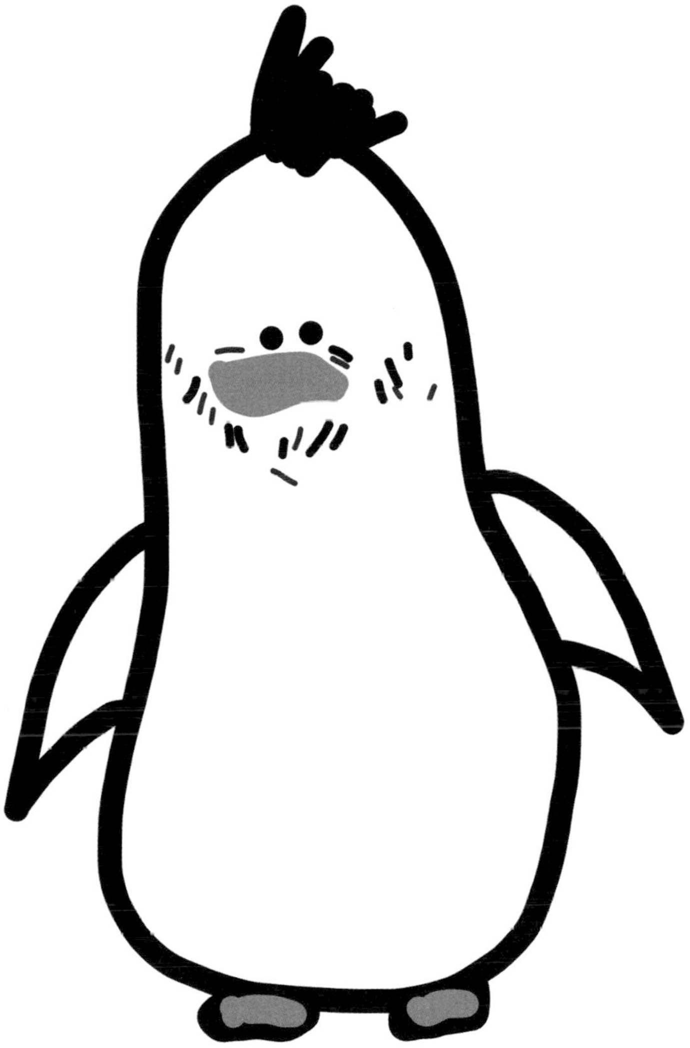

*N*ever-Ending Sweat Loop: The term for when you get clean, but then you get hot while you're drying your hair, so then you need a shower again, ad infinitum.

Serving a cocktail in a mason jar and calling it "artisanal" doesn't make it worth $21. But it does make you notice that it's spelled "art is anal."

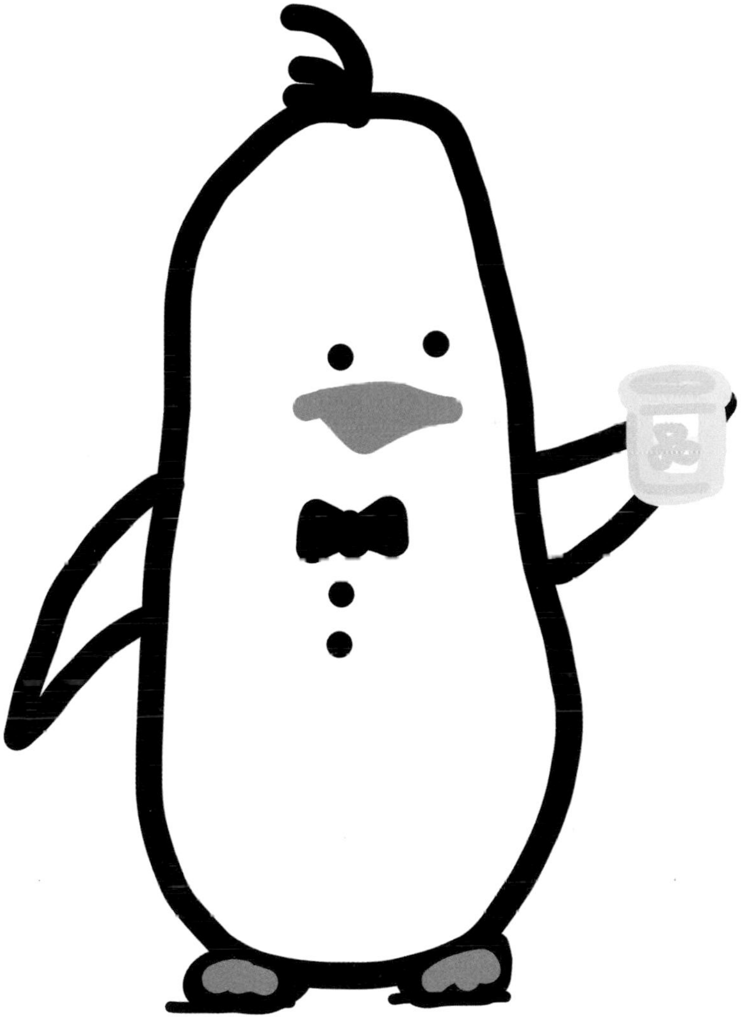

Halfway through changing clothes, Patty became trapped half-in and half-out of her dress, and now she fears she will die and be found this way.

You may think you're pretty smart—but Dwayne filled a pita pocket with ice cream, so he's a genius.

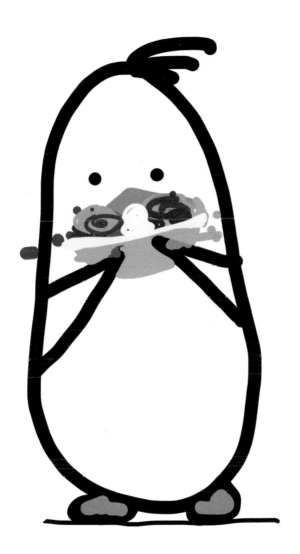

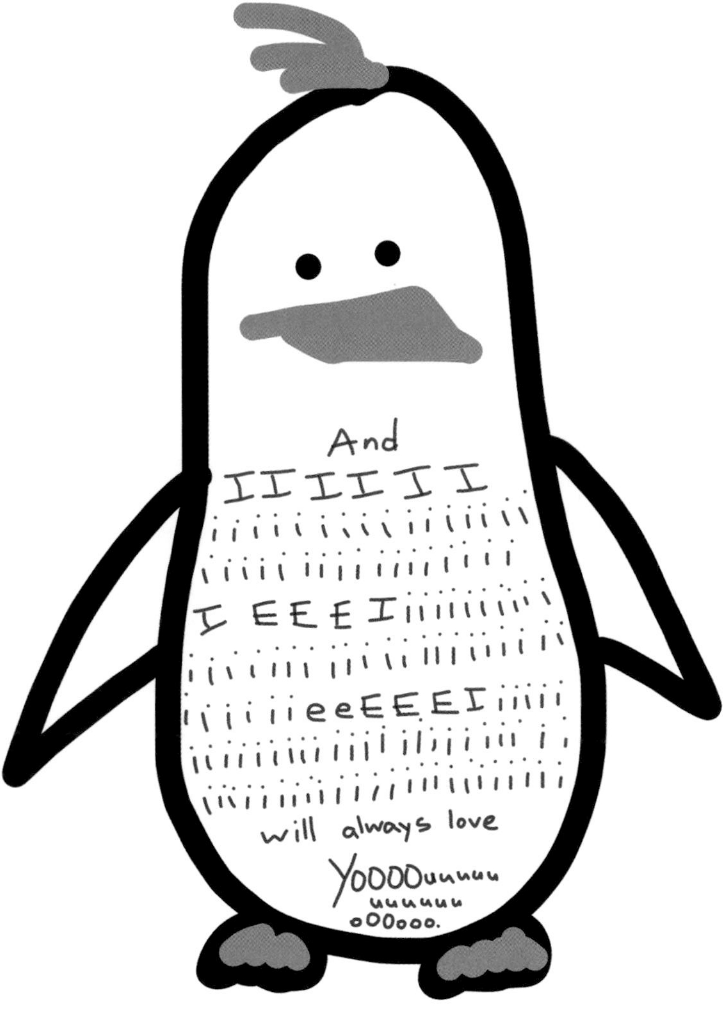
And
IIIIII
I EEEI
eeEEEI
will always love
YOOOOuuuuu
uuuuuu
oOOooo.

He'd heard the way to look cool was to get a tattoo of a favorite song lyric.

ACKNOWLEDGMENTS

First of all: Big love to JP, plus WC, MG, Mom, Dad, and my whole family. To my best friends—you know who you are—and all the early supporters of "The Random Penguins," thank you and an inappropriately long hug with an uncomfortable amount of eye contact.

Extra thanks and a flippity-flappity hug to Kristyn Keene and the folks at ICM; Meg Leder, John Duff, Amanda Shih, and the gang at Perigee Books and Penguin Random House; and everyone at Parnassus Books.

ABOUT THE AUTHOR

Mary Laura Philpott has written for the *New York Times*, *The Toast*, and *The Queen Latifah Show*, among other outlets. She is the social media director for Parnassus Books in Nashville, Tennessee, and the editor of *Musing*, its literary magazine.